Life's A Journey, Are You Packed?

Life's A Journey, Are You Packed?

LIVING AND THRIVING WITH JUVENILE
RHEUMATOID ARTHRITIS

Stefanie Foster Freeman HHC

ISBN: 1535595558
ISBN 13: 9781535595551
Library of Congress Control Number: 2016913789
CreateSpace Independent Publishing Platform
North Charleston, South Carolina

In loving memory of my mom and dad
Audrey Elaine Foster and Robert Stanley Foster

Chapters

Dedication

I dedicate this book to Audrey Elaine Gootman Foster and Robert Stanley Foster, Mom and Dad. I am beyond thankful that our souls chose each other. You both taught me so much. Unconditional love, compassion, kindness, generosity and the love of family. You guided me through my JRA journey. You never made me feel like I was sick. I had a wonderful childhood full of love and fun. Seaside Beach Club in the summers and UConn basketball in the winters.

Thank you for loving my kids and instilling your values in them as well. Everyday when Samantha and Alana have a decision to make, I know they think, what would Nana and Papa do. We all live our lives to make you proud.

I wish you were here to see how hard I have worked to heal myself and start a business to help others. I know how proud you are, I just wish you were here so I could tell you, and hug you one more time. I wish that I knew then, what I know now, so I could have used all of these resources to help you heal. I love you both always and forever.

"If heaven wasn't so far away, I'd pack up the kids and go for the day." Justin Moore

Acknowledgements

I want to thank so many people that it may be longer than the actual book. First and foremost I must thank my parents for their love and support through everything. Although they were both gone much too early, their life lessons live on in me. Their confidence and faith in me has led me exactly where I am today.

Samantha and Alana thank you for being amazing and supportive daughters. Being your Mom is truly the greatest blessing. We have been through so much together, hard times, many losses, but many happy memories. We laugh, we argue and we push each other to be our best version of ourselves. You have seen me struggle with my pain and were always just there to love me. Thank you for always supporting me in all my various endeavors, especially writing this book. You both give me more joy then you will ever know. I love you both and I hope that my journey helps you both live your healthiest most authentic life.

Kyle and Kris thank you both for your support. Any crazy idea I had you always said, "Yep Stef you can do this." Del thank you for supporting me in our marriage and now. We may have an unusual family we created, but it's our unusual and it works.

Chris thank you for loving me, for me. You just get me. Every time I came home and said lets try this food or that food, you always figured it out for me. You call restaurants before we go to make sure I can eat there. You have created recipes for me so that I can enjoy healthy savory food. You are an amazing cook. You immediately jumped on board with me and essential oils, as you saw how we all benefited from them. You have trusted me as I continue to study and seek a healthy path for us. When I told you I was writing a book you said, "You got this Stef, it's going to be a great book." Your trust in me means more then words can say. Lindsey, you have only know me for a few years, but I appreciate your trust in a healthy lifestyle as well. I'm happy to have you on the essential oil journey with all of us.

My brother Stu, thanks for listening to all of my ideas on how to get healthy. We saw Mom and Dad go through so much and I know you're on this journey with me. You have always been my cheerleader from day one. Even when I made you and your friends leave the driveway so me and my friends could play.

To my friends: my lifelong friends, my college friends, my South Windsor friends, my IIN friends, my oily friends, my Fitness 19 friends, my in-laws and all my cousins, you are too many to name, but just know that you have made an impact on my life. I love you all so much.

Joshua Rosenthal, Lindsey Smith and Sue Brown thank you for IIN, the amazing book writing class and making my dream of writing a book come true.

To all my doctors from my diagnosis to now. I thank every one of you for helping me along my journey.

Let's all reach out to each other when in need and help each other live our healthiest, most authentic life. I am thankful for my illness for it has led me to my life's passion, helping others. If this book touches one person's life and leads them on a healthy journey, it will have served its purpose.

"I believe that the greatest gift you can give your family and the world is a healthy you." Joyce Meyer

How I got the name of the book

I was on the phone, with my best friend BJ's mom, telling her about my book writing course and some vague ideas of what I was going to write. She had no idea she was giving me the name of my book, but she did. She asked me if I remembered a saying she had hanging up on her refrigerator when I was 6 or 7 years old. I responded that I couldn't remember what I ate for lunch that day. She said on an 8 1/2 x11 sheet of paper with a black background and white writing, there was a quote that I would read every time I went over there to play. She told me she knew I didn't understand what it meant at the time, but I had to read it every time. It said "Life's A Journey, Are You Packed?"

I shrieked and said OMG Karen that's it!! That's the name of my book...and so it began. Hugs and kisses to you Karen for the name of my book and for blessing me with my bestie.

What is wrong with me?

How old are you in your first childhood memory? I was 3 years and 9 months old, Thanksgiving 1969.

I was so excited as we pulled up to Aunt Sylvia and Uncle Ozzie's house in Newton Highlands, MA. As my dad pulled up in front of their house, my brothers ran out of the car almost before it came to a complete stop. They were already in the house as my dad followed with the containers of yummy food my Mom had prepared. I was sitting in my big, bulky, blue booster seat, the kind with the bar contraption that pulled over your head (like on a carnival ride) and locked you in. I guess by that age I was able to get myself out, because my mom poked her head in the car and said "Come on Stef." I couldn't move. Listen I was three years old, I have this memory, but couldn't tell you how I was feeling or what I thought. Of course the story was told to me by my parents, but I vividly remember the day. Apparently I could not walk and was complaining of pain in my right hip.

I was carried around all that day by everyone and I loved it. I am the youngest child, "the baby." I have two older brothers, who at the time were 13 and 10. My parents never panicked, at least

1

not in front of me; they just said we'll take you to the doctor on Monday.

Monday morning we went to see Dr. Guss, my pediatrician. He told my Mom that I had "water on my hip" and sent me to the hospital to get it drained. Apparently, the pain subsided and I was okay until a few years later. I had "water on my knee." Back to the hospital I went to get it drained. The problem was that it kept happening. As I was growing, I had more and more weird pains that were classified as growing pains. When I was eleven years old, I remember being at Dr. Mason's office, my pediatric dentist. He kept asking me to open my mouth wider. I was explaining to him that I couldn't because it hurt and kept clicking. At the time, I also had a brace on my wrist that he asked about. I told him the doctor gave it to me because my wrist was hurting. We walked out into his waiting room so I could pick out my "prize" from the treasure chest. I overheard him ask my mother if I had gone to any specialists for all these aches and pains? She said we had been to an orthopedist, allergist, pediatrician and nothing.

Backing up a bit. I was sick all the time with sinus infections and strep throat, which meant I was on A LOT of antibiotics. The doctors thought maybe I had Lyme Disease or rheumatic fever that was cured from taking all these antibiotics. The problem was, the pain wasn't going away and new joints were swelling and hurting every day.

I could tell by this point it was hard on my mom that I was in so much pain. We went to discuss it with the pediatrician again. He was such a kind-hearted old man. When I say old, I mean he was in his early 60's, not really that old. At that time, to me he was old. At this appointment, he took my hands in his hands palms up, and looked at me and then my mother and said "I know what

2

she has…I think it's Juvenile Rheumatoid Arthritis." He showed us the red spots on the palms of my hands under the skin. He told us this is a sign of JRA. Mrs. Guss heard us and came running in. She hugged me and said "Oh Steffie you're going to be alright I promise." They sent me to the hospital to get blood drawn and promised they would call as soon as they got the results.

We were upset, relieved and hopeful all at the same time. My Mom said let's go get a tuna sandwich at Bee Bee Dairy Bar and an ice cream sundae at Friendly's in Norwichtown. Here began the food as a reward cycle. No fault of my Mom; she's a good Jewish mom and food solves everything right?

A week after Dr. Guss had his epiphany, a Friday I vividly remember, we got the results. I came walking out of the side door of Thomas W Mahan Elementary School and got into the car. My mom looked at me very matter of factly, said Dr. Guss called and you have JRA. I need to take you to a Rheumatologist, but I can't call until Monday.

A week later, we drove to Hartford, Connecticut, to see a rheumatologist. I was scared but happy to hopefully get some answers. I just remember, unfortunately, he was very short with us, scared us and we cried. That very day my Mom called my relatives in the Boston area and found the name of "the best JRA specialist" at Brigham and Women's Hospital in Boston, MA. Dr. Patricia Fraser was a doll. I guess this is how we did it before the internet - call your relatives.

When I started seeing Dr. Fraser I was taking tylenol. Clearly it was not helping. She spent hours with us, testing all my joints, taking X-rays, drawing more blood and going over all of our options. By the time I got to her, the pain had spread to my back and ribs. It had spread to every joint, from my jaw down to my ankles. Sitting was very difficult, so I spent a lot of time laying down. She decided to put me on a medication called Arthropan, an anti-inflammatory. The first thing my mom asked was about side effects. She explained all of them. She felt that although there were many side effects, I absolutely had to start on the medication to try to slow down the process. She told my mom, but not me at the time thank goodness, that when you have JRA you either go into remission by age 16-18 or it could ultimately be deadly.

What is juvenile rheumatoid arthritis? It is an inflammation of the joints where the joints get swollen, warm and painful. Almost 300,000 children in the United States suffer from some sort of arthritis. It can be short-term and last for a few weeks to a few months or it can be chronic and last for years. In about half of the cases it can last a lifetime. There are many different types of JRA. I had polyarticular arthritis, rheumatoid factor positive. This type behaves most like adult rheumatoid arthritis. Kids with this type of arthritis are at a higher risk of joint damage than other forms of JRA. There is no known cause of JRA. It is an autoimmune disease. The immune system is supposed to protect the body from harmful invaders. However, with an autoimmune disease, the body releases chemicals that can damage healthy tissues and cause pain and inflammation. The doctors have found that the more joints that are affected, the more severe the disease and the less likely it will go into total remission. JRA is now called JIA, juvenile idiopathic arthritis (kidshealth.org Juvenile Idiopathic Arthritis).

The medication helped a little bit, but the disease was going from joint to joint. Staying ahead of the pain was tough. For me, it was my new normal and I didn't really share much with my friends.

Honestly I didn't know what to say. In seventh grade, the year of my Bat Mitzvah, was the toughest year. I missed forty-five days of school. My parents had to take me back and forth to Florida throughout the winter. The warmer weather helped my joints. My mom was brought up in Miami Beach and her best friend Char lived in Hollywood, FL. There were no complaints from me spending time in Florida and visiting Char. I look back on my childhood and feel very blessed. I had amazing parents and friends. To me I had an idyllic childhood with this pesky disease. I spent a lot of time at home and a lot of time with my parents.

June 15,1979, the big day!! The Friday night before my Bat Mitzvah. I was so excited, I had spent many years studying and I knew my Haftorah like the back of my hand. The best thing was that my mom said I didn't have to go to school on Friday. I was having a relaxing morning watching TV with my mom, when all of a sudden I got a bloody nose. It happened to me a lot because of the medication, only this time it wouldn't stop. After a while my mom took me to the hospital where I had to have my nose cauterized. They gave me some medication for the pain. However, I had to back off my anti-inflammatory medication, because of the bleeding. I got home from the hospital just in time to get dressed and head to Beth Jacob Synagogue. Apparently I did an amazing job. At least that's what my parents told me, but I felt like I was in a fog. I got up Saturday morning, June 16, 1979, ready for what the day had in store for me. My nose felt better, but from backing off the meds, I was in a good amount of pain. Who had time for that? I put on my white floral sundress with the pretty green jacket, as I had to have my shoulders covered on the Bima. The piece d'resistance of the outfit was the pink eyelet lace up espadrilles. I guess my love for shoes started at an early age.

I made it through the day and had a wonderful time at the evening celebration with all my friends and relatives. Everyone came from near and far to celebrate this special time in my life, which was such a blessing. It certainly took my mind off what I was going through.

Ages 11-13 were the most difficult ones for me with JRA. When I was in eighth grade, my Mom broke the news to me that I may not be able to go to Norwich Free Academy (NFA). It was the local high school. I was devastated because I wanted to go with all my friends. It was a really cool high school that was set up like a mini college campus. Every building had several floors and no elevators. At this point getting out of bed was hard, never mind walking up and down stairs. We looked into some private schools, but I was adamant that I was going to NFA, and I did. Fortunately as the time grew near, I started feeling a little better. By the time I was sixteen, I had what would be my last appointment with the doctor in Boston for many years. As she examined me she asked what my pain level was. When she reviewed my blood work, there was no sign of medication. I said it seemed better. She thought I may be going into remission, but still wanted to change my medication. There was one problem, a side effect from this new medication was Glaucoma. My Mom looked at me and said "Can you deal with the pain?" I nodded my head yes and the decision was made, no more medication. Hugs for the doctor and bagels and ice cream to celebrate. At 16, I was in some type of remission. It was hard to determine at this point if it was temporary or permanent. I thought this was the end of my ordeal. Boy was I wrong.

High school was pretty uneventful with my JRA, but I was constantly sick. Chronic tonsillitis, sinus infections and allergies. I was just so happy to be at NFA with all of my friends. I was a good student and like all other high schoolers, I loved having fun with my friends on the weekends. Unless of course I was traveling to the UConn (University of Connecticut) basketball games with my parents.

My one true love, from an early age, was UConn basketball. Through my Dad's real estate business, he formed a friendship with the Athletic Department at UConn. We had season tickets to all the men's basketball games, home and away. I spent my down-time studying the stats of all the players. It was at a young age that I decided I wanted to be a sports writer. I worked at the Norwich Bulletin, in the sports department, my junior and senior years of high school. I loved going to the games. After the games my Dad would take me down to the hallway outside the locker rooms and the players would come out to talk to me. Tony Hanson, Corny Thompson, Karl Hobbs, these guys were amazing and always happy to spend time talking to me about the game. This was my focus, not my pain. As an adult I have been able to reconnect with many of the players. How cool is that? In fact in 2005 I was asked to do a TV commercial for college basketball and Coca Cola. Our family friend Jimmy, in the athletic department, told me a group of UConn board members were at a meeting looking for someone to be in the commercial. They were looking for a woman basketball fanatic that had a family. Jimmy said we all looked at each other and said "Stef Foster." We taped it in December and it aired during the 2006 NCAA tournament. A total dream come true.

I remember being at a specific game with my Dad at the Hartford Civic Center. The Huskies were playing Syracuse. Big game, but I had tonsillitis and a fever of 101. I went anyway. At the end of the game my Dad nudged me and said "Hey Stef, we only lost to Syracuse by thirty points, we are getting good, you watch." Well the rest as they say is history and I still love my Huskies.

In remission - sort of

Junior year was full of PSAT's, SAT's and college visits. I knew I wanted to be a sports writer, but I also wanted to go to school in a big city. My dad wanted me to go to UConn in the worst way. He offered me a brand new car, a condo, jewelry, you name it. I was such a homebody. The thought, even at age 17, of being away from home and my parents, terrified me. I wasn't sure if it was just who I was or that my illness played a part in this. I knew in my heart if I didn't leave home and go to college a good distance away, I never would. I applied to UConn (back then the local safety school), Boston University, Villanova, Boston College and Tufts. I really wanted to go to BU. When my mom asked why, I told her the shopping in Boston is awesome. I could also go to the theater whenever I wanted. She laughed and told me I was going to be a college student and shopping and the theater wouldn't be in my budget. Really?? I hadn't thought about that. March of 1984 and everyone was getting acceptance letters. My best friend Barrie Jill (we called her BJ) got her acceptance letter to BU and so did a few other friends. I was stressed out. Would I get in? I had great grades and decent SAT scores. Why hadn't I heard? My mother was also a bit nervous. One morning she strongly suggested that we go do a last minute trip to Syracuse. It was, after all, the number one communications school in the country. I said no way!! I was adamant!! We were in Syracuse for the 1981 Big East Basketball tournament and it was so cold I had to buy an extra hat, scarf and gloves. Even all of that didn't protect me from the blistering wind and cold. I told her it was too cold and I hated it there. I made her happy and sent in an application. I was accepted and well, yep you guessed it. She ignored me and planned a trip to Syracuse. The day before we were leaving I called my friend Gail's brother. He was a freshmen there and I asked if he would show me around. All the while thinking, there's no way I'm going there, but let me appease my parents.

On a Friday morning in March we loaded up the car and off to Syracuse we went. After a six-hour drive, we pulled up in front of my friend's dorm. I grabbed my stuff, got out of the car and shut the door. I tapped on my mom's window. When she rolled it down I said "I'm going here." Why?? I can't explain it, but it just felt right. I eventually got an acceptance to BU. Although it would be hard to be at a different school then BJ, I had to do it.

August 1984, I packed up all of my stuff and headed to the land of the orange. We pulled up in front of Day Hall on Mt. Olympus where the unloading began. I was on the first floor in a one-bed-room share, but we did have our own bathroom. My parents helped me get all my stuff set up. Then it was time for them to go back to Connecticut. I walked them out and hugged first my mom and then my dad. I shed a few tears but knew this was the beginning of the rest of my life. What a wonderful opportunity my parents were giving me, a college education. Well my dad hugged and hugged and hugged me and cried and cried. My mom rolled down the window and said "Bob get in the car; stop making a scene." Off they drove.

I went into my room and was blasting Springsteen. The next thing I know, a girl named Amy walked in and said "You like Springsteen, so do I." She was my first friend in college. We are still the best of friends. And I still love Bruce Springsteen. I have seen him in concert about sixty times. Music has and always will feed my soul.

During the first semester, I really felt like I was hitting my stride. Well socially, not academically. I remember going into the lecture halls and getting a syllabus that told you the homework assignments and tests. I thought wow I can just do all of this work on my own time. Do I really need to go to every class? Well first semester was over and I went to every football game, knew all the best bars and places to shop...but when my report card arrived, I had a 1.4. I was on probation in Newhouse. I intercepted the letter, so my parents never knew. Okay first semester jitters done, time to buckle down.

I went back in mid-January 1985. I was determined to have a much better semester. Within a week I was so sick I could hardly get out of bed. I dragged myself to the infirmary. The diagnosis was mononucleosis. Academically it was a blessing in disguise. All I could do was go to class and study. End of semester two and I had a 3.8. I was back in the good graces of Newhouse. By my sophomore year I learned how to balance academics and fun. Syracuse was absolutely the right choice for me. I have the most wonderful, amazing friends that remain by my side to this day.

The summer of 1987 was the summer before my senior year. It was the last hurrah before I would get a real job and be an adult. BJ, Gail and I (friends since age 2 in Nursery school) went to the beach all the time. We were having such a fun summer.

One morning in July, as I was packing my beach bag, BJ called me to tell me she wasn't ready yet. She actually wasn't feeling that well. She needed a little more time to get ready. A few hours went by and I hadn't heard from her. The phone rang, but it was her mom Karen. She said, honey we had to take BJ to the hospital-her left side felt numb. A CT Scan showed a bleed in her brain. She may have been born with it, but she will need to be watched and have some physical therapy. I went to see her as soon as I could. A few weeks went by and she wasn't improving. Karen called me to tell me she had searched the country for the best neurologist. She found him at Yale New Haven Hospital, so that's where BJ was going. After several tests, they found she had a brain tumor the size of a baseball. This was a life-changing moment. We were 21 years old and my best friend had a brain tumor. It could not be true. Her surgery was scheduled for a few days later. I went to visit her and I will never forget what she said. She said, "Stef if I die please take care of Jen (her sister)." I looked at her in disbelief and said "BJ, you are NOT going to die. You better not die, because if you do I'll kill you. You can't leave me." A month before that we were concerned about what bikini we were going to wear to the beach. Now we were talking about life or death. Boy did that put everything into perspective. Even though I had suffered with JRA, to me it wasn't a life or death situation. But this was.

The surgery went well. As I arrived the day after her surgery, Karen was at the door greeting all her visitors. She said "Anyone that doesn't have a positive attitude can't visit." I walked in to see my best friend, my true soul sister, lying in a bed, head shaved with a scar from the front of her head to the back. To me she never looked more beautiful. She was alive and that's all I cared about. I told her to hurry up and get better. We had a lot to accomplish in this life. She was truly amazing. She took off one semester. She returned to school in January of 1988 and graduated only a semester late.

I was right when I said we had a lot to accomplish. She was in my wedding party and I, in hers. Our kids call each other Auntie. Although we never lived near each other again, we talked sometimes every day, sometimes every few days. I can honestly say I would not be the person I am today without her by my side. We were there for each other no matter what was going on in our lives. When our kids were young and life was so hectic we had a standing date to chat. We would both go to Dunkin Donuts for coffee, at the same time every morning, in our respective towns. That was our time to catch up. Different cities living similar lives. She was on a healthy living path for her and her son long before I was.

Time for the real world

Upon graduating from SU I had a rude awakening. I thought when I graduated with a degree in Newspaper Journalism from Newhouse School of Public Communication, the Hartford Courant was waiting to hire me. I was ready to be the UConn men's basketball beat writer. Well that just wasn't the case. I decided to head to New York where my friends were living and give it a go. I had several interviews, one at Sports Illustrated for a position as a reporter. A few days later I got the call of my dreams!! The woman on the other end of the phone said "Stefanie we would like to offer you a position as a reporter with Sports Illustrated." The next day I got the call of my nightmares!! "Stefanie I am so sorry, I was too quick to offer you the position, my boss just informed me that we had to hire from within." Great just great. No job living in NYC. Back to job hunting. I finally landed a job as an administrative assistant at a home fashions magazine. I lasted for about a year and threw in the towel. It wasn't my dream job. Certainly not dream money, so it was time to go home and regroup. I moved back home briefly. I worked in retail management then moved back out. In 1990, a friend of mine asked me if I would be the manager of her new all-natural cosmetic store, in a new mall in Manchester, CT. I took the position that would lead me to the beginning of my journey as an adult.

One of the girls I worked with, asked me if I wanted to go on a date with her brother. My boyfriend and I just broke up so why not? We met and started dating a few months later. Looking back, he was nice and honestly I wasn't thinking about forever. My parents met on a blind date, got engaged seven days later, and were happily married. That seemed like a good formula.

In December of 1990 we got engaged. To say my mother was upset was an understatement. He was divorced, Roman Catholic, ten years older then me with 2 children. Not exactly what she had in mind for her little Jewish girl. However, after she said her peace, she accepted it, because he was a nice guy. She then went a step further and told me not only was I marrying Del, but his two kids would be mine. She said "I don't EVER want to hear you refer to them as your step-children, they are your kids and our grandchildren." I learned so much about myself. I loved these boys from day one, like they were my own.

We were very different, but I thought, opposites attract. Not always. We married in 1991. I had always wanted to be a biological Mom as far back as I could remember. If truth be told, I dreamed of daughters. In May of 1992 I had a UTI and was taking an antibiotic. At the same time I was taking Motrin for my joint pain. I went to work one morning and ended up in the bathroom with severe pain in my abdomen. My boss called me an ambulance. Fortunately, my gynecologist met me at the hospital. He told me that my kidneys shut down from a combination of the antibiotics and motrin. He also said I had a horrible case of endometriosis and I probably would not be able to have children. I was devastated, yet somehow had a feeling he was wrong.

I knew in my heart I was going to have kids. After a few months of not conceiving, I took a round of clomid and conceived. We were thrilled! You would have thought the day I found out, a green light of eating went off in my head. After trying to eat well and keep my weight down for years, all bets were off now. Hostess Donuts for breakfast with skim milk of course. McDonald's french fries for lunch and the list goes on. Considering the JRA, my pregnancy went pretty well. I went into labor on October 17, 1993 at 10pm, while watching Pretty Woman." As I walked into the delivery room, the nurse asked me to step on the scale. I replied with "Can my husband wait outside?" I tipped the scales at a hearty 214!! I am 5'2" on a real good day. I thought, well, I'm having a baby so I'll be about 150 tomorrow. Haha that was funny. After hours and hours and hours of labor at 1:42pm on October 18, 1993, Samantha Renee DuFresne, was born. I was over the moon and completely in love with her.

My mom would come and stay with us to help me with Sam. In January 1994, she spent the night with us. The next day she headed to Florida to visit Char. When she and Del left for the airport, I began to cry. I wasn't sure why until the next day. That afternoon I went to meet with my boss to decide on a date I would return to work. I was selling advertising, part-time, at the local newspaper. When I pulled into the garage, Del came running out and said, "Your father was in a car accident and they don't know if he's dead or alive." He was alive thank goodness. He just hit his head and blacked out. Otherwise he was only banged up and bruised. We didn't know at the time this caused a domino effect on his health. This was the day I realized how I was connected to my Dad. This wouldn't be the only incident like this.

Again, I tried to get pregnant. This time, two doses of clomid and I was pregnant. At this point, it still had not dawned on me that something in my body was not functioning properly. I had no idea what alternative medicine was, so I never looked for answers there. I had thankfully returned to my pre-pregnancy weight before I conceived a second time. That was still overweight and unhealthy. I only gained eighteen pounds this time. The final three months I was so anemic. Someone had to be with me most of the time, as I could sit down and fall asleep immediately. At 5am on November 23, 1995, Thanksgiving Day, I went into labor. At 4:04pm Alana Michelle DuFresne was born. When they handed her to me I looked at the nurse and said "That's the same baby as last time." They looked so similar and here I was again, completely in love with my 2nd daughter.

I came home the next day. Through the next week I wasn't feeling well. I just chalked it up to having a new baby and a 2 year old. By day 7, I had a high fever and the pain in my abdomen was excruciating. Del took me to the doctor in Hartford. When I walked out of the office crying, it totally freaked him out. I had a pelvic infection. They wheeled me next door to the hospital. Del had to take the kids home. I was on heavy-duty antibiotics and stayed in the hospital for 72 hours. I laid in that hospital bed for 3 days and cried. I couldn't be with my newborn. I had to pump and throw out the milk until I was off the antibiotics. My 2 year old was missing me and I felt guilty leaving Del to handle everything at home.

When those three days were over, I was back home with my family. The JRA would sneak up on me but not every day. I decided as the girls were growing up that it was time to get my weight under control. I was in pain and exhausted. Here was the start of my yo yo dieting.

When low fat foods were introduced I thought that was the key. I did not realize they took the fat out and added other junk.

So this train of thought didn't work. I decided to try another diet-no sweets and count calories. So Sunday night before starting, I thought it would be a good idea to eat everything I would ever want, as if it were my last meal. Pop tarts, hot fries, smart food popcorn, starburst jelly beans and many other yummies.

Monday was a good diet day, because I was so nauseous from the day before. By Tuesday afternoon I fell off the wagon. Okay, so new plan. I should start the following week on Tuesday! Maybe that was the trick because I stayed on that diet for a month. Then I fell off the wagon again. I could not lose weight! I tricked myself. I would eat bagels, but dug out the middle to save calories. I would only have a handful of jelly beans. Eat well all week and cheat on the weekends. Clearly I had no idea what I was doing. I just wanted someone to tell me exactly what to eat and when. So off to Weight Watchers. This wasn't the first time I tried WW. Every meeting I went to was so inspiring. So many people lost so much weight. When they started talking points, I would think to myself "Stef, you have a college degree, but these points are too confusing to figure out." What was wrong with me?? I would beat myself up, but I just couldn't succeed. Looking back I understand why. I was not honest with myself. Most important was that mentally I was not ready.

In 2000, I decided I needed to hire a personal trainer. That was very helpful for me physically, but I still had a hard time with my eating. I was able to lose about 10-15 pounds. More important, I really fell in love with exercise.

Balancing a family and parents

From the time my dad was in his car accident in 1994, he and my mom had several health issues. He first had prostate cancer. A few months later he started having some issues with his memory. He was finally diagnosed with Parkinson's Disease. When my dad had surgery for his cancer, my mom decided it was time to focus on her health. She lost 40 pounds and started exercising. Shortly after my dad recovered, my mom had a heart attack. She had 3 stents put in her arteries. This prompted her to become even more diligent about her eating and exercise. A few years later she had a melanoma on her shin that required major surgery and a skin graft. At this point, I was going back and forth an hour each way to Norwich. I would do their errands and grocery shopping to help. In 2001 I finally convinced them to move closer. They built a house five miles from us and I couldn't have been happier. Through all of this our love for UConn basketball got us through. It was a fun way to divert our minds from all this illness.

From 1988 on there were so many fantastic memories connected to UConn basketball. Who could have predicted this? Just my Dad. NIT Championships, Big East Championships and four

NCAA Championships. The most amazing and heart-warming memory for me was the very first championship in 1999. I went with my parents to the Final Four in St. Petersburg, FL. It was UConn, Duke, Michigan State and Ohio State. Duke beat Michigan State and UConn beat Ohio State. The final game would be UConn and Duke. Wow, I never thought this could happen. My parents had been going to games since 1953. To hear UConn mentioned in the same sentence as Duke, made them giddy. I vividly remember standing in the lobby of the hotel, chatting with a guy from Waterbury we knew from the early 70's. He said he remembered me as a little girl and couldn't believe I was a Mom now. We chatted excitedly about the game and how far the Huskies have come in twenty years. He told me he had a hunch. He wrote a message on a piece of paper. He folded it up and handed it to me. He said not to open it until after the game. So I made a promise. We walked over to the arena. A few moments later it was tip off. The game was a nail biter from start to finish. My parents were sitting a few rows behind me, to my right. When the final buzzer sounded the score was 77-74. The University of Connecticut Huskies were crowned the champions. "They shocked the world." I turned and looked at my parents. They were hugging and kissing and crying and laughing and jumping up and down. I don't think I had ever seen them so happy. It made me cry. Every family has their own activities they do to connect. Ours was UConn basketball. I ran up to join in on the hugging and jumping and screaming. My dad asked if I looked at that piece of paper in my pocket. I said "oh no I forgot about it, let me look." I took it out and unfolded it. It said 77-74 UCONN. Wow, he knew. I found out that a few months later he had passed away from a long illness. I can't remember his name but his face is etched in my memory forever.

My parents loved their new house and settled into life in Ellington. They had lived in Norwich for close to 50 years. The girls loved going over there to visit. It was much easier for me to help them. One morning in October 2001, I woke up and just started to cry uncontrollably. Del asked what was wrong? He asked if I was sick or PMSing? I told him I honestly had no Idea why I was crying. I just couldn't stop. About two hours later, my Dad called me frantically looking for my Mom. She was at the dentist, so I went over to see what was wrong. He told me he fell in the shower. Of course I blamed it on him not eating breakfast. I tried to give him peanut butter on a bagel, which in hind sight, was the worst thing I could have done. We brought him to the hospital to get checked out. He fell in the shower because he had suffered a stroke. Fortunately no permanent damage. However, because he had Parkinson's, he just became weaker overall.

By 2004, my dad, the strongest man I know, needed full-time help. I don't ever remember him being sick when I was a kid. He was running 5K runs into his 60's. He loved acting, singing and performing in many plays. My Mom called me one morning crying to tell me she just couldn't do this alone anymore. She and my Dad wanted to move in with us. We checked with the town to see if we could make our house handicap accessible. The town said we could not. We built a new house with a handicap accessible in-law suite. The back of the house was all windows, so my Dad could be inside, but see the kids playing outside. In May 2004, we all moved in to Vintage Lane.

It was such a wonderful blessing for all of us to be able to share every day. It wasn't always easy, but I would not have had it any other way. My kids had to see their grandparents go through some tough health issues. The wonderful memories certainly outweigh the sad ones. February 22, 2005, after five bouts of pneumonia, my dad passed away at age 75. I was in denial for a long time. I knew he was sick, but he was my Dad. The first man I ever loved. My basketball buddy. The man who stood at the front of Day Hall and cried when he had to leave. Now he left me for good. He left a huge hole in my heart. The lessons of love and kindness will live in my heart forever. When sad, what do I turn to? Food. I stuffed my feelings down with food. The more I ate, the worse I felt, but I couldn't stop.

April 2005, off we go to Ocean Isle, NC for a much needed vacation. We vacationed with several other family friends from South Windsor. I remember walking into our rental house when Del's phone rang. It was his Mom; she was just diagnosed with lung cancer. We hadn't grieved for my Dad yet and now this. At this point I was just sad for my kids. Shortly after we returned home, we moved her into the rehab center my dad had been in. She went downhill quickly and passed away July 27, 2005, at age 71. Two deaths in five months. The loss and raising a family of 4 kids was surely tough. Tough on our physical and emotional health.

In May of 2007, Del's Dad died from a multitude of health issues at only 72. Six weeks later we got another blow. I got a call from Del's sister. All she said was "Georgette is dead. She was in a car accident." Georgette was Del's dad's wife. Sixty-one years old and gone in an instant. In two years, my kids have now lost 4 grandparents. How do you rationalize this? How do you move on? Somehow we just moved on without really dealing with our feelings. We didn't even realize the damage our denial was beginning to take on us emotionally and physically. Three years later we lose my mom. Five years of loss.

Really? How did this happen?

March 7, 2010, the beginning of the most life-changing event for me. It was a Sunday morning. When I got up, I walked the long, plant-filled hallway, down to my mom's area of the house. I said "Hey Mom what's up?" She said "I am having horrible pain in my back and down my legs." I said matter of factly "It's probably your sciatic like you had last year when you had the epidural shot." She looked at me like I was speaking a foreign language. I just dismissed it and asked if she needed anything. I then went back down to check on the girls. A while later, as I was getting ready to visit a friend that had just had ACL surgery, she limped down to our area. She announced that she may need to go to the hospital. I said "Mom, really? For back pain?" We always made fun of her, in a loving way of course. The ambulance had our house on cruise control. I called my Mom the sickest healthiest person I knew. She loved to go to the doctor, just to be reassured that she was healthy. Just a month before her cardiologist told her he wished he would be as healthy at 78. Her Dad and two brothers dropped dead in their early 50's, so I totally understood her anxiety over her health, but low back pain?

Off I went to visit my friend. As soon as I got there, Mom called me and said she needed to go to the hospital. Sam was at home so I had her dial 911. I rushed home. I followed the ambulance to the hospital. I have spent many days and nights with both my parents in the ER. I had determined that no matter how quickly they came in to see them it was a six hour ordeal. When I met my Mom in her room, she was just different. I couldn't figure it out. I figured it was because she was in so much pain. She had such a high tolerance for pain, but I had never seen her in so much pain.

At 1am, the doctor finally came in to tell me to take her home. I looked at him and said "Excuse me? She's writhing in pain, you gave her morphine and you expect me to take her home? What did the tests show?" He said nothing. I asked if they did an MRI and he told me no they didn't feel she needed it. I asked what her temperature was and he said she doesn't have one. I asked if he could please tell me the number? He replied it was 98.9, not a temp. I told him I was her caregiver. Her normal temp runs about 97 and 98.9 for her is a fever. He dismissed me and sent in an aide. When the aide came in to get her to stand up, she collapsed to the floor. Her legs couldn't hold her up. I went out and found the doctor and pleaded with him to let her stay through the night. I needed to figure something out fast. He at least agreed to that.

First thing Monday morning I called the rehabilitation center my Dad had been in and spoke to the director. I explained the situation and begged him to give my Mom a room. He said he remembered my parents and of course would give her a room. He did explain that due to the fact that she wasn't being transferred by the hospital, I would have to pay out of pocket. I said let's do it. My mother took care of me my whole life and I would do anything to get her well.

When I arrived at the hospital an hour later I walked in as the nurse was asking her where she was. She answered the bank. The nurse said what are you doing at the bank? My Mom gave her a look and said getting money what else would I be doing at the bank? I took the nurse aside and said what was that all about? She was at the gym Friday, Talbots on Saturday, back pain yesterday and now she has no idea where she is? The nurse said it's called delirium and many elderly people get it in the hospital. I thought nope not buying it. My Mom is the smartest woman I know and there is something else going on.

I set up an ambulance to transport her to the rehab center. I went home to get a little sleep. My older brother called me in the afternoon. He said that he had the strangest conversation with my Mom. She asked him when my other brother was going to be visiting her. He told her that he was on the way and should be there within 30 minutes. She said "How could that be? Have you talked to Stef? She took me to Florida and it's much farther then 30 minutes away." I jumped up and headed to see my Mom. As I walked into the room, my friend who was a physical therapy assistant interning there, was assessing her. She said this is not like your Mom. What is going on? I was at a loss.

The next night the doctor called to inform me that Mom spiked a 102 fever. They were sending her back to Hartford Hospital. I met her there and they admitted her to the hospital. Still no MRI, no tests. She was adamant about going to Hartford Hospital because all of her doctors were based there. Guess what? They no longer had hospital privileges. She would have to see a Hospitalist. Well I met with said hospitalist and yep wasn't impressed. Friday afternoon, when I was visiting with her, she knew who I was but had no idea what was going on with her. She called it "the deal." She would say "When are they going to figure out this whole deal?" As

I left to go pick up Alana from her 8th grade trip to Washington, I asked if I could bring her back some food. Her eyes lit up and she said "Yes please a tuna sandwich from Au Bon Pain." I returned at about 9pm with the sandwich. She was asleep so I left it in the refrigerator. She never ate the sandwich, she never ate much more. That evening another middle-of-the night call from the doctor to tell me she spiked a fever, went into Atrial Fibrillation and may have a pseudo bowel obstruction. They moved her into ICU and called in an infectious disease specialist. I ran over to the hospital to talk to her new doctor and beg for an MRI. Nope he said. It's not necessary, it's her bowels and we are working on that, I was told. At this point I was less then nice. I firmly told the doctor that she arrived almost a week ago with back pain. It doesn't take a rocket scientist to figure out that maybe this is all stemming from her back. Again no. My brothers and I were told that we had no idea what we were talking about.

A week later a neurologist was called in on the case. She came in to the room and said she needed to speak to me. She asked if my mother was paralyzed? She told me that she has no feeling and can not move her legs. I said well she wasn't paralyzed when she got to the ER two weeks ago. She wanted me to sign a release form to do an MRI of my mom's brain. I said NO!! That's right NO!! You will do an MRI of her back today. She looked at me and knew I was serious. I was done with the run-around and the horrible system. She was wheeled down 30 minutes later for an MRI.

The next day my siblings and I were called into a meeting where we would get the MRI results. The results were that my mother had an infection in her spine that spread to her brain. She would never walk again and she may not live. That was like a punch right in my gut. Really?? An infection in her spine? What if she had the MRI the day she came into the ER with back pain? We were devastated and fired all kinds of questions at the head of neurology. Here was his brilliant response "I understand how devastating this is for you but those questions are over the tips of my skis." Really?? Over the tips of your skis? I wanted to take said skis and bash him over the head with them. For the next 6 weeks she was kept comfortable on antibiotics and pain meds. I truly believe in my heart that she lived as long as she did to give us all a chance to say goodbye and make peace with it the best we could.

April of 2010, my Mom had been in the hospital for a month at this point. Going to the hospital every day and sleeping there many nights had taken it's toll on me. After repeatedly going to doctors and having them tell me that my RA factor and the blood work didn't show active arthritis, I decided to call in the big guns again. I searched and searched and finally found a number for Dr. Patricia Fraser. I called her office to make an appointment. The receptionist informed me that she only worked one day a week and she wasn't taking new patients. I told her I wasn't a new patient. I just had not been there for about 30 years. She told me she would double check with the doctor, but not to expect a call back. Twenty minutes later she called me and asked if I could come in next week. Yay, I thought this appointment was finally going to help relieve my pain.

That next week I took the trip from Connecticut to Brigham and Women's Hospital. I was crying all the way there, remembering the many trips I took with my mom. Well now I was going alone. Now she was in a hospital, in ICU, on a ventilator. I whispered in her ear the night before and told her where I was going. I know that's what she would want me to do.

I arrived at the doctors office and they took me in to see her. She looked at me, hugged me and said, "When the receptionist said Stefanie Foster is trying to make an appointment, I said I will see her." She remembered me. She remembered that my mom and I used to come see her every week, "How could I forget," she said. I wish the appointment went as well as the reception she gave me.

After X-rays, blood work and an exam, her conclusion was that the JRA had done a number on my joints. I was, at this point, 190 pounds. My blood pressure was 148-90 and I couldn't get out of bed without taking Alleve. She strongly recommended I take Enbrel (a biologic drug) to stop more damage. I pleaded and said "I'm not ready to give in to this disease." I really didn't want to be on a drug for the rest of my life, but I did want to have a quality of life. We finally agreed that I would take Naproxen and see how I did on that. She also suggested I take Zantac coat my stomach. The Naproxen did help my pain, but I had to have blood work to make sure it wasn't affecting my liver. Herein lies my problem, on a drug for inflammation, but it can cause other problems. I saw my Mom live this way for years and I refused to do the same. There has to be another way. I stopped taking it. I would take over the counter anti-inflammatories only when I couldn't stand the pain.

After 2 1/2 months of watching my Mom, my best friend, struggle, I questioned everything. The whole medical system. The medical staff would not listen to me and had no answers.

I knew I had to take another avenue to get to wellness. For years my family and I had looked to traditional medicine and it really didn't work for us. I started realizing that my parents were prescribed so much medication to basically "put out fires." I was wondering why they never got to the root cause of the illness. That's such a thing isn't it? My Mom had high blood pressure, so they gave her a pill to bring it down. Why not find out what's causing it?

I had all these questions, but where could I get the answers? How I was going to change my path was yet to be determined.

On May 28, 2010 at 10:10am, after I told my Mom what an amazing Mom she was and that it was time for her to go be with my dad, she took her last breath holding my hand. She was 78 1/2. I didn't think I wanted to be with her when she passed away, but she made the choice. It was the most precious gift she could have ever given to me. She was there on the day I entered this world. I was there with her on the day she physically left this world.

Grief leads to life change

As you can imagine, this took a toll on my body. My joints were so painful that I couldn't get out of bed without taking three Alleve. Taking care of my health was definitely not a priority at this point. After my Mom passed away, it completely changed me. I knew I had to take control of my health but honestly I didn't know how. I was casually smoking, drinking at least a six pack of diet pepsi a day and was completely sad and unhappy.

They say you shouldn't make major decisions until a year after a loss. Well a month later I told Del I thought we should move to Virginia. I had several friends in Chesapeake, VA, and I fell in love with the area. Frankly, I needed a change and fast. I needed to get out of the house I shared with my parents. Going down to their area of the house without them living there was too much to handle. In 2006 I first went to therapy to sort out some things, figure out who I was and what I wanted. I went back to the same therapist to figure out what my new normal would look like…Life without my Mom.

In July 2010 I found a lot in Chesapeake. The building began in November 2010. I knew Del was not really on board with the move south; he was a northern guy. Over the next few months we had some very tough talks. We were both so completely broken over all the loss and were not sure we could heal together. Anytime you go through tough times it's hard. Instead of growing together we grew apart. Those differences were there all along; we just ignored them until it was too late. We separated in 2011 and got divorced. I moved to Virginia and he moved to a cabin in the woods of Vermont, which was always his dream.

When the house in Chesapeake was almost built it was time to put the pool in. I met with the pool construction guy and picked out the liner, brick coping and concrete color. After meeting a few times and chatting about the pool and college sports I called BJ to tell her I just met the male version of me. I found out much later that the pool construction guy (Chris) called his friend Greg and told him that he met the female version of himself. We both apparently had a strong emotional connection. In the summer of 2011 our friendship turned into a wonderful journey. We quickly realized how alike we were. We had so many similar interests: sports, music and travel.

In January 2012 I was feeling very settled in Chesapeake, VA. I knew it was time to find a gym and get moving. Enough being fat and happy. My joints were on fire and it was time to focus. I joined Fitness 19 and signed up for three personal training sessions. I told Tony, the owner, that I had a few bad experiences with trainers at gyms. I had some physical limitations and wanted the best trainer he had to offer. He assured me Jared would be perfect for me.

A few days later I called Jared to make an appointment. When I showed up for my first session I remember walking towards the scale, as he was asking me questions. I explained about my JRA. I also told him about my workouts with a few awesome trainers in

Connecticut. I wanted to lose maybe 10-15 pounds. He said okay. I know, in his head, he was thinking lady you have WAY more then 10-15 pounds to lose. I weighed 197 pounds. The first few appointments we were getting to know each other, but we soon became comical relief for the rest of the gym. We fight, we argue, we swear at each other the whole time and by we I mean I do. He kind of nods his head and says okay but that has nothing to do with you working hard so get going. When I complain, his famous line is "I don't even understand what that means."

I lost about 10-15 pounds by December 2012 and was feeling good. It wasn't until I changed my lifestyle in May 2013 that I started hitting my stride. I made the food changes. However, without Jared and his gentle prodding, I would not be where I am today. He is very knowledgeable with a degree in Exercise Science. He knows exactly how to push me to my limits without me getting hurt. When I do come in with an injury, he adjusts and keeps me moving forward. He has me do workouts that even people without JRA couldn't do at my age. My workouts consist of intense cardio and lifting. All kinds of fun stuff that he makes up. Once in a while, he gives me accolades, but not often. When I moved to Virginia Beach I didn't know what I was going to do. I decided to stay at Fitness 19 and drive the 35 minutes to work out. I knew I couldn't replace Jared (shhh don't tell him that- he's cocky enough). Fitness 19 is my fitness family, from Jared, to the owners, other trainers, and members that I see there all the time. It's where I feel comfortable. It's where I thrive.

Chris and I were married December 28, 2012 at the Hilton Oceanfront Virginia Beach. Getting married without my parents was such a weird concept. My older brother walked me down the aisle and my children all stood my my side. My brother Stu gave a wonderful speech on behalf of my whole family.

As I was in the bridal suite, just before I walked down the aisle, I got a text that brought tears to my eyes. It was from Del and it read "I hope today is a great day for you. You were a wonderful wife and are an amazing mother and you deserve to be happy." What a blessing to get a text like that from your ex-husband. We had a lot of tough times, but were able to move on. One person is not responsible for a divorce and I'm so proud that we were able to accept what was and move toward the future and work on ourselves.

I have no regrets. We have four amazing kids and as Del said "We had a good 20-year run." It took a lot of self-reflection on both of our parts, but I'm happy to say we are friends. We share not only our kids, but wonderful memories. He was a fabulous son-in-law to both my parents, taking care of them like they were his own. He comes to Virginia to visit the kids and stays with us. He and Chris get along great. It's not a "typical" family situation, but it's our "normal." He seems very happy in Vermont and has a wonderful support system. For this, I am thankful.

It certainly wasn't easy to mesh our families. Chris has one daughter, so with my four and his one, it was hard on the kids at different times for sure. They all ranged in age from 17-28. No little kids, but hard none the less. My kids all realized how happy we were and how happy Del was in Vermont. I believe they all understand and for that I am eternally grateful.

My life in Virginia with Chris and the kids made me more and more hopeful every day. I started to understand that my Mom passing away set me on a path that I never could have ever imagined. I was born and raised in Connecticut. I never, ever, thought of moving to another state. Sometimes the universe has other plans for you. I guess I'm lucky I was open to these plans, because the following years have been quite an amazing ride so far.

The doctor that saved my life

After spending my whole life trying to live with the pain of JRA and it's damage, I saw a post on Facebook. It was a post from Stu's childhood friend, who became a chiropractor. It said "Cold laser treatments for your knees to help arthritis pain." Boom…here's my answer. I googled chiropractors in the area that offered cold laser treatments. I found a chiropractor/naturopath at Norfolk Chiropractic Center. I called and made an appointment for a complete check-up two weeks later.

I walked in very confident that I knew what I needed. Sitting in the exam room I was thinking that I really had it all together. I mean I work out, eat pretty healthy, wear a size 14 (tried to block that out) so he'll probably just give me the treatments. Then I'll be on my way. Ummm no, I was completely wrong.

The doctor walked into the room and introduced himself. He asked me some questions about my health history. I confidently told him that I had JRA, I exercise, eat healthy and I just need cold laser treatments. Then I'll be good. He smiled and stated "Mrs. Freeman I'm the doctor, I will do a complete exam and some X-rays. I'll tell you what we are going to do. And by the way, everyone thinks they eat healthy." Yikes...now I was a bit scared. The X-rays showed damage in my joints and osteoarthritis in my neck. I stepped on a machine to be fitted for orthotics. When I asked if he was going to X-ray my knees, he told me from the look of my neck and feet he knows my knees are bad. He then sent me to the lab to get several vials of blood drawn for extensive blood work. I had an appointment to come back in two weeks-April 30th.

April 30, 2013...the day that changed my life. The doctor walked into the exam room with all the information I had been looking for since I was three years old. Every other doctor I went to always tested my RA factor along with other levels for my arthritis. Here is the thing, my JRA went into remission, so it's not active in my body. However the autoimmune disease still lives in my body. I think other doctors didn't really have any answers for me (my opinion only) so they recommended surgery for my joints, anti-inflammatories to manage the pain and biologic drugs. FINALLY I found someone who listened to me and dug deeper. Okay so here is the blood level that set me on the road to feeling better...the CRP, Cardiac reactive protein level. It should be less then 1.0 and mine was 3.77, YIKES!! What does this mean?

I was completely inflamed. At this point I still didn't really understand what this meant, so I asked. He said heart disease, diabetes and cancer. Inflammation is the root cause to all disease. I looked at him and thought HOLY I need to fix this now!! But how?

He handed me a pamphlet for an anti-inflammatory lifestyle. He started me on some supplements: vitamin D, Magnesium, a probiotic and omega-3. Before I continue with my journey, here is one lesson I learned. There are doctors out there to help you, but ultimately it is up to you to choose your path. As I walked out of his office in a daze I knew EVERYTHING had to change, but what and how.

That evening Chris and I met some friends at California Pizza Kitchen before a Bob Segar concert. I still hadn't decided what to do, but that is the only thing I could think about. While Chris and I were walking out of the concert he said he didn't think his voice was that good. He hated our seats. They were on the side and we had to keep our heads turned to the left all night, so annoying. I looked at him with a glazed look in my eyes and said huh? All I thought of all night was "I'm 47 I can't die, I'm 47 I can't die." We got home at midnight and I told him he needed to help me. I flipped through the pamphlet and decided at that point what I had to do. I said I'm not going to worry about what I can't eat, I'm going to focus on what I can eat. I was not going on a DIET! Why would I want to embark on a journey that began with the word DIE. I decided I would make a LIFESTYLE change. That was better. Start something that began with the word LIFE.

Chris is an amazing cook so I knew I could count on him. I made a list. I could eat organic, local and grass-fed chicken, fish, meat; organic and locally grown fruits and vegetables; nuts, beans, organic dark chocolate over 72% and red wine. NO sugar, NO gluten, NO dairy (other than organic greek yogurt) and NO PRESERVATIVES, nothing in a package. I literally went to Harris Teeter and said goodbye to all the foods I would NEVER eat again. No going halfway on this, no cheat days, I decided on this very day that I was all in. Goodbye to triscuits, wheat thins, hot fries, sour jelly bellys, starburst and sweet tarts, just to name a few.

Well on May 1, 2013 my new lifestyle began. Honestly when it became about my health and not about fitting into a certain size, it was easy. After 3 weeks I started to feel better. As each day went on I felt better and better. I was eating healthy and working out harder. In July I had a little physical set back. I got up off the couch to go to bed and stopped in the kitchen to get some water. I turned around and had this excruciating pain in my right knee. I hobbled to bed and began to cry; I thought I tore my ACL. I saw many basketball players make a sudden move, fall down and boom. Seriously I was feeling better but comparing myself to an athlete? I may have lost my mind. I hobbled in to bed and said to Chris "I'm just feeling better, losing weight, working out hard and now this, what am I going to do?" After a few minutes he calmed me down and said "Stef I doubt you tore your ACL walking across the kitchen, but tomorrow morning I will drive you to the chiropractor." The pain subsided and I fell asleep. I awoke at midnight, got up, took two steps and literally crawled into the bathroom. Two steps in and I had this pain down my left leg that was like nothing I have ever felt. It felt like hot flames shooting down the inside of my whole leg. I hobbled to the toilet and sat down. I screamed out for Chris and said "I need your help." I stood up and the next thing I remember is him lifting me on the bed saying "seriously can you help a little?" I guess when I lifted my head he saw my eyes roll back in my head. It was then he realized I passed out. He said he thought I had a stroke and it scared the heck out of him. I knew it was nothing like that. I felt fine it was just that pain in my leg.

First thing in the morning we headed to the doctor. I could barely walk without help. The doctor examined me. He said he didn't think it had anything to do with my knee. He assisted me and told me to squat. Down I went, but the pain was in my back, not my knee. He said if it was my knee I wouldn't be able to squat. His diagnosis was pain from my sciatic nerve. I laid down on the table and he used an apparatus that essentially shot into my butt cheek. As if that wasn't enough, he dug his elbow so deep I thought

I was going to cry from the pain. When I got up off the table I did a full squat and walked out. How about that?? No shot, no drugs, no surgery. An adjustment and I was at the gym the next day. I became so obsessed with finding alternatives. This was just the beginning of my journey.

The one thing that never wavered was my commitment to eating healthy. Six months in and I was down 40-50 pounds (just a guess I NEVER go on the scale). My CRP level dropped to .65. I felt so amazing that I wanted to shout it from the rooftops. I was ready to help anyone and everyone. At this point, I was trying to figure out how to make that happen.

Now eight months in and time for new clothes. I went to see my friend at White House Black Market. The last time I had purchased a pair of jeans there, they were a size 14. Surely I'm down a size or two I thought. When I walked in he said "OMG what are you doing you need some new clothes." I had a ball as he kept bringing me stuff to try on. What size did I buy? I bought some tops size small or 4 and pants in size 2 and 4. What the what???? I didn't wear that size on the way up. I kept checking the tag. The smallest I have ever worn as an adult was a size 6 when I was in my early 30's, on a crazy diet. Actually I was only a size 6 in the dressing room because I never actually wore the size 6 jeans. I will tell you, yes I was proud to be a much smaller size, but what really mattered to me was the fact that I was getting healthier every day. My joint pain was pretty much gone for the first time since I was three years old. At this point I adopted the saying "Healthy feels better then food tastes."

I sat down in that dressing room and cried. I cried for all the hard work I had done up until this point. I cried that it took me until 47 to figure this out and get the help I needed. I cried that my parents were not here to see me. To celebrate with me. I cried that I couldn't help them with their health. It was then that I knew I was here and went through all I had, to help other people. Then I smiled, a big smile, knowing that they are watching over me and are so proud of me. They are with me on every step of my journey. It is from their strength that I get my strength.

Out I walked, with my multiple bags, ready for the continuation of my journey. The one thought that kept running through my mind was "how do I get my message out?" I started a business called "finally fit forever." I did a blog post on my Facebook page. I talked to friends and family, but I knew there was a better way to get my message out to the public. I just didn't know what it looked like yet.

One night Chris and I were at dinner. There was a girl in her early twenties, with her parents, sitting next to us. She was crying about her joint pain, migraines and she wanted to take a semester off from school. Her parents seemed to me like they were frustrated with her and it broke my heart. Chris gave me the look and nod that it was okay for me to say something to them. I said "Excuse me, I didn't mean to overhear your conversation, but it struck a chord with me. I think I might be able to help." They all looked at me and said "really how?" I told them briefly that I had JRA. I explained that I found a doctor who helped me. He helped me heal through changing what I ate. I gave her his name and number. The daughter stood up with tears in her eyes, hugged me and said thank you. When we got in the car to leave, Chris said, "I can see that this is your passion. Your eyes light up and you get so excited to help people. Now you just have to figure out a way to get paid for it." I thought, hmmm, he has a good point about the paying thing. At this point, I had done a lot of research and had a ton of knowledge about nutrition and auto-immune diseases. However, who wanted to pay someone with a degree in Journalism from Syracuse University, who was a sales rep for a gift company. This was the million-dollar question.

My ah-ha moment and IIN

A few weeks later was my ah-ha moment. In 2014 we decided we were going to sell our house in Chesapeake, VA. We were ready to move to the beach, in Virginia Beach. We went to the beach almost every Sunday to go to open houses. We also drove around looking for empty lots. We decided 2015 was the year we would move. We went to the Home Show at the Virginia Beach Convention Center in March 2015. We were wandering around getting ideas when we came upon a women selling Aloe lotion. It was just Aloe, nothing else in the lotion. Chris said he was buying it for his dry hands. I started chatting with the woman selling it, no surprise, I can talk to anyone. She was telling me that she was from Charlottesville and this was her part time job. It was some extra money, while she got her Health Coaching business going. I looked at her and said "A Health Coach?? What is that and how do I become one?" She told me that she went to the Institute of Integrative Nutrition, an online program, based out of New York City. I turned around and said to Chris, "I need to do this; lets go home!!"

When I arrived home that Friday night, I googled the Institute of Integrative Nutrition (IIN). I signed up for a webinar the next morning. Monday I called to sign up for the course that began the following week on March 16, 2015. This was yet another life-changing event in my journey.

To say that IIN was life changing, is for me the understatement of the century. The course was set up into 40 modules over a year. You had one week to listen to lectures and study each module, about 15-20 hours a week. In my heart I believe everyone would benefit from going through this program, regardless of your career path. Many people attend IIN to help themselves with their own health journey.

I always thought, can you really learn with an online course? Do you feel part of a community? Do you get the help you need? OMG a resounding yes to all of these questions and more. Before the course even started, a Facebook page for March 2015 students was launched. We all introduced ourselves and quickly became friends, virtual friends. When you have a common goal and are like-minded, it doesn't take long to form amazing friendships.

Six weeks into the curriculum we were encouraged to reach out and find an Accountability Coach. What is that? A fellow student that will hold you accountable and vice-versa. You are supposed to touch base once a week to help with studies. You are encouraged to bounce ideas off each other as you move along in your health-coaching journey. Memorial Day weekend 2015, I was on the Facebook page and saw a post from a student looking for an accountability coach. I read what she had to say and it resonated with me. I immediately sent her a message. You know how certain events happen and you remember exactly where you where? Well I got her response when Chris and I were walking on the boardwalk. We messaged back and forth and decided to talk on Tuesday.

On that Tuesday we spoke for over two hours about everything. I told my story first and then she told hers. We were laughing so hard, because when we told our stories, we knew exactly what happened on what date. So I would say my Mom got sick on Sunday, March 7, 2010 and she spoke in the same way. We knew from that first conversation that our connection was something called Synchronicity. Joshua Rosenthal, the Founder of IIN, taught us about Synchronicity. Synchronicity is a term coined by Carl Jung. It refers to the subtle interaction between an individual and a universal force. I know for sure the universe brought Johanna and I together. This simple word explained so many things in my life.

Through IIN I learned about many different eating styles. I heard lectures from some very famous people in the field of nutrition. The one phrase coined by Joshua is "Bio-Individuality." There is no one right way of eating for everyone. Each person is an individual and one person's medicine (referring to food) can be another person's poison. Each person must be treated differently. Not only is the food you eat important to nourish your body, but your primary food is equally important. IIN taught us all about Primary Foods. Primary Foods are healthy relationships, regular physical activity, a fulfilling career and a spiritual practice. This nourishes your soul while healthy food choices nourish your body. After learning this, everything became clear. I can fulfill my purpose in life. I am now equipped to help many different people by just listening to them and treating them each as individuals.

Every day on my journey I was feeling stronger physically and mentally. Then I had another minor setback. These setbacks are just part of learning to live with JRA. I deal with them head-on and make changes to keep moving forward. The pain was again in my right knee radiating down my leg. It was both hard to straighten and bend my leg. At first my chiropractor thought it was coming from my sciatica again. When it just wasn't getting better he referred me to an orthopedist to get a diagnosis. He thought it was a torn meniscus.

Off I went to the orthopedist. It was a very efficient office. They called my name, took X-rays and put me into an exam room. The doctor walked in, introduced himself to me and said "Do you want the medical diagnosis or can I be a straight shooter?" I said oh please be a straight shooter. First he asked if I had ever had X-rays of my knees. I laughed and told him, yes many times. The next thing he said was "Stef, your knees look like crap and you need double knee replacements yesterday. Quite honestly I'm not sure how you are walking around, let alone working out." I told him it was my lifestyle. He said he had to believe me because there was no other explanation. I also had a torn meniscus. Due to the condition of my knees, surgery (not that I was going to consent to it) would not work. Now the discussion turned to treatment. First suggestion was double knee replacements and to that I replied no thank you. He asked me to please think about it. He said if I make it to 55 without it to consider myself lucky. I said to him, "oh doctor you don't know me." When I set my mind to something, I will persevere. Setbacks are the story of my disease. It's how you push through and overcome them that is the key. The second suggestion was a steroid shot. To that I replied "My mom died from a shot in her back that I believe caused her infection, no thank you." The third suggestion was an anti-inflammatory, no thanks. I said there has to be another option. Well there was, physical therapy. I said okay sure I'll do that. This, I will come to find out, was another life-changing path for me. We parted friends. He said please contact me when you are ready for the surgery; it's come a long way. I told him he was a great guy and thanks but no thanks.

Physical therapy here I come. Day one assessment…torn meniscus and an SI joint that pops in and out. I completely connected with Michele my physical therapist. I didn't know, that in a short time a suggestion from her would give me new tools for my health journey.

Six weeks, three days a week of exercises and ultrasound. Michele and Mike were my therapists. One day while having ultrasound on my knee I was telling Mike that the doctor told me I could never do squats again. I didn't understand why not. I would have to sit in a chair for the rest of my life. He said you know what, you're right. So I started slowly again with Jared. No weight on my back. I was back to squats in no time. They pushed me and by the end of six weeks I was back to normal, well my normal. Michele suggested I also try yoga, hot yoga at that. I laughed and said with my hot flashes, hot yoga sounds like the last thing I would ever want to do. I did buy a Groupon to try gentle yoga. I fell in love with yoga. I made it part of my practice two days a week. The life changer at physical therapy had nothing to do with physical therapy. I was telling Michele about my horrible hot flashes. I explained that I was unwilling to take anything. She told me she met a girl, Jenn, who sells essential oils. She had just started using them and loved them. She thought maybe that would help. I went home and emailed Jenn. We made an appointment for the next day.

Young Living essential oils-Game changer

I told Sam and Alana that I was going to talk to a women about essential oils and I thought they may also be beneficial for them. So the three of us went to meet Jenn. I had seen some Facebook posts about essential oils. I tried to google them and find out what they were all about but to no avail. Well all that changed at Jenn's house August 8, 2015.

Jenn's story: She's 39 years, tried getting pregnant for 5 1/2 years. For many years she lived a healthy lifestyle, yoga, healthy food, herbs and supplements. She went through fertility meds, IUI's and was at the point of IVF. For her it just didn't feel right. Many of her friends were reading Facebook posts by another friend, Celeste, about Young Living Essential oils. Being the self-proclaimed science geek that she is, her friends asked her to do some research and see what she thought about Young Living. She was currently using a different brand and was ashamed to say it was very much inferior to Young Living. She and her friends all purchased a kit to use for their families. The first oil that blew their minds was Thieves. Their kids came home from school sick, they put it on the bottom of their feet and the next day they got up feeling fine. WHAT?? No trip to the doctor? No missed school days? Definitely a WOW. One day Jenn was helping a friend going through menopause and every oil for menopause also said for fertility. She thought, how could that be, two totally different ends of the spectrum. Well with more research she realized that these oils support your body in balancing your own hormones to where they need to be. She started on a three month regimen of these hormone balancing oils and…Baby Nate was conceived. Everyone was in shock especially her fertility doctor. In November 2015 she delivered a beautiful, oily, Lemon Droplet (see paragraph on next page about the Lemon Droppers) baby Nate. This story literally blew my mind.

Back to our meeting at Jenn's August 8th. She talked to the girls and I about the oils and the benefits for our specific concerns. Hot flashes, overall immune boosting, joint pain, anxiety and sleep. She ran a zyto scan (a scan that tests the biomarkers in your body to see what specific products you need) on all three of us. The top two oils that came up on mine was an oil called brain power and one called Oola friends. Brain power is for, among other things, people that have a family history of alzheimer's and parkinson's disease. Bingo! Friends is exactly what it sounds like, it brings like-minded friends into your life. Friends affirmation: "I am blessed with empowering, healthy relationships."

I bought a starter kit for myself and both girls, along with the specific oils we each needed. Sam said don't waste the money on one for her, but something in my gut told me this was going to be life changing. Being a health coach Jenn suggested that I look into the business end of Young Living and explained to me about an amazing group I would become a part of called the Lemon Droppers. It all sounded great but I shut her down immediately and said, nope not interested. I dabbled in a different MLM company lost money and thanks but no thanks. She told me that she was going to stack (whatever that meant) the girls underneath me just in case. I told her to stack away but it will NEVER happen. She handed me an extra starter kit she had so I could get started right away and when mine came in I would give her that one. Well that kit she handed me sat on my table for a week and a half. I looked at it a few times, felt overwhelmed (I should have called her but I didn't). When the girl's kits came in they immediately started diffusing and so I finally opened my kit and I never looked back. After two days of diffusing and applying the oils for hormone support I called Jenn and said, "What is this crack, I need more and I need to share with everyone." Yep she knew me better then I knew myself. I watched the videos that explain every step of the way how to become a Lemon Dropper and I haven't looked back. She was right, the oils pair so well with my health coaching business. I finally understood what "stacking" meant. It meant that my girls would be my business partners in this oily journey and we will all make a sustainable residual income forever as we help people begin their own health journey. I can't think of anything better then this. And Sam, who didn't want a kit, never leaves her house without her oils.

What is a Lemon Dropper? It is a super cool, amazingly awesome subsection of Young Living. It was started by two geniuses Lindsay Teague Moreno and Monique McLean. They figured out how to be successful in this world of network marketing. They put it all out there on social media. The premise of this group really resonates with me. We don't sell; we educate people about essential oils. I have NEVER been involved with a group of such amazing and inspiring people that only want to live their most healthy, happiest life along side like-minded people.

In September 2015 I decided I would have a get together, with Jenn's help at my house, to spread the oily love. The first person I felt compelled to share these oils with was Johanna from IIN. The problem was that we have had many conversations about "other" companies and how people shove it down your throat. They aren't always that educated about the products they are selling. It took me a few weeks to get the courage to call her and talk about Young Living. When I finally did I said okay girl hear me out. I know in our previous conversations we said we would never sell things BUT please listen to what I have to say. I spoke so fast I was surprised she heard a single word. As I held my breath, Johanna said "Stef, if you are this passionate about it, I trust you and I will buy a kit and try it." I said really? Really? Yay you are going to love this and what it will do for you and your family. I'm proud to say that she is on this amazing journey with me and I couldn't be happier. She has experienced so many life changing moments from the oils, but that's for her to tell in her own book someday:).

Oils have become my way of life. I use 12-14+ everyday. Hormone balancing, stress relief, highest potential, abundance, build your dream, brain power and friends to name a few. I diffuse brain power and clarity any time I do work, like writing this book. When "friends" came up on my zyto scan the girls said, "Mom seriously you have more friends then the two of us put together." I do have so many wonderful friends. My best friends from childhood, my college friends and friends from South Windsor. Since I moved to Virginia I hadn't really met any like minded people. Well all that changed with my coveted bottle of Friends. I met more friends then I can count through this business. Is this a coincidence or a connection? There is a connection. Put it out in the universe and it comes back to you.

I spend every day educating people on how they can benefit from these little bottles of awesomeness. I have met some amazing friends from all over the country. I have built an incredible team that I love. The support from those that started before me is second to none. For me IIN and Young Living have the same philosophy and for me are intertwined. I have two women on my team in Singapore that I met through IIN. How cool is that?? If only I had a private jet to visit all these people.

Health conference dream

I n October 2015, Chris and I met Johanna at the "Take Back Your
Health" health conference in Alexandria, Virginia. The woman
who put it on was a graduate of IIN, who also suffered from JRA.
I was able to meet another IIN graduate who healed a goiter on
her thyroid through whole food, Andrea Beaman. She is my girl
crush. I loved listening to her speak about her journey and how
she healed herself in a similar way. I, of course, took a picture with
her and bought all of her books. When I got in the car, I looked at
Chris and said I want to do this in Virginia Beach. How? I had no
plan yet but I knew I'd figure it out. I knew in my heart that I had
to tell my story to help other people suffering with auto immune
diseases. People want to know they are not suffering alone. They
want to connect. I have always pictured myself speaking in front of
a large group of people. In fact when we were at a Darius Rucker
concert, he sang his song "This" which is about life events that
happen or don't happen that all bring you here to this. My favorite
part of the song goes like this "How I cried when my mama passed
away, But now I've got an angel looking out for me today, So nothing's a mistake, It led me here to this." I looked at Chris and said
when I walk out on the stage of the Staples Center in LA some day,

I want this playing. He just chuckled and said dream big or what? Crazy thing is, he knew I was serious. He just gets me.

Remember Synchronicity? Yep it struck again. In March 2016, I was at the Green Cat meeting my oily friend Beth, also an IIN graduate, from North Carolina. We were talking oils and business. As we got up to leave, I heard someone say Stef. I turned around and looked at this woman and said hi, thinking to myself who in the world are you? She said "It's Nicole I planned your wedding at the Hilton." The face looked familiar, but when she planned our wedding her hair was short and dark. This woman looking at me had long platinum blonde hair with bangs. Eventually it clicked. Sometimes you have a connection with people, but maybe when you meet them the timing isn't right. Honestly you can't stay in touch with every single person you meet and connect with. Trust me I certainly try. Obviously I looked much different as well. She asked what I was up to. I told her I was a health coach and an essential oil educator. She told me she had started her own wardrobe consulting business. We exchanged business cards and planned a meeting for the following week.

Our first of what I'm sure will be a lifetime of meetings was so much fun. We both talked excitingly about our businesses. I told her my dream of speaking in front of a large group of people about my journey. I want to empower people to take control of their physical and emotional health. She loved my idea and asked if I would be willing to partner up with her and move forward with a seminar. I said YES! Let's do this. Out of our next meeting evolved our business Valor & Vibrancy http://www.yourauthenticselfseries.com. We had so much fun coming up with the name. I was telling her, that since I have gone on my health journey, people say to me all the time that I am glowing or I am vibrant.

We decided on a derivative of vibrant…so vibrancy. She wanted to use another "V" word. We came up with a few and then she asked are there any oils that begin with "V"? I said yes, only one of the best most amazing oils ever, called Valor. What is the definition of valor? Courage or bravery, strength of mind or spirit, personal bravery. Ding ding ding we have a winner!! It is called "chiropractor in a bottle." You can use it in the morning for a positive attitude or at the end of the day to unwind. We use it for pretty much everything. From this discussion Valor & Vibrancy was born.

Valor & Vibrancy presents Your Authentic Self Series. What is Your Authentic Self Series? This is a women's health series focused on educating women on ways to improve or change our daily choices in order to live the healthiest life. YASS will be offered as an ongoing seminar series where local leaders in the health/wellness and beauty industry will excite you, inspire you and motivate you to be the best version of you. The first seminar will be in Virginia Beach at a local private school, with local speakers and 20 local vendors. Our long term goal is to have these going on around the country and then around the world.

"So many of our dreams at first seem impossible, then they seem improbable, and then, when we summon the will, they soon become inevitable" Christopher Reeve

As the title of the book says "Life's a Journey, Are You Packed?" To me this means life is honestly a journey and you can never stop working and growing, on your health, both physical and emotional. As my journey continued here is another synchronicity encounter. My dear friend gave me a gift certificate for my 50th birthday. It was for a facial at a place I had never been. It took me several weeks to get an appointment, so I knew she must be amazing. After meeting the esthetician she and I would become fast friends. We chatted almost the entire time. I told her about my journey and she told me about hers. In fact, she said that she had just told me her whole life story and she never does that. I said yep I tend to have the affect on people, maybe it's my journalism degree. Then we both laughed. When I left, of course I rebooked as it was amazing. She gave me a business card of a functional medicine doctor that she went to and thought I would love her. It took me a few months but I finally emailed the doctor. I had been searching for a doctor that was on the same page as me. I thought I found one in Alexandria, VA until I met this one. She is a chiropractor, acupuncturist and functional medicine doctor.

She spent three hours with me at my first visit. She could tell I had mononucleosis previously by looking at my tongue. She did my blood type and many other tests. The diagnosis was viral over-load and adrenal fatigue. JRA has really done a number on every cell in my body. I have an A positive blood type. So I went home and read up on it. People with my blood type usually do best with a vegetarian style of eating. I adopted a pescatarian lifestyle and I felt even better. No meat and no chicken. When she originally asked what meat I eat, I told her a lot of chicken and a small amount of red meat. She said chicken is tough for me to digest and that it causes a lot of phlegm. A light bulb went off in my head. I told her I am always clearing my throat!! I have been trying to figure out what caused all of my phlegm. I knew it couldn't be the tiny bit of lactose-free cream I put in my coffee. See if you keep searching eventually you get lots of answers.

She said my pulse points are weak which means very low energy. I looked at her with an odd look and said I feel like I have so much energy. She said compared to what? She explained that I had been so sick for so long that I have no idea what it means to have energy. Wait a few months and you will have this unbelievable grounded energy that will be very foreign to you she explained. I thought okay sounds great bring it on.

The next test she suggested was genetic testing. I sent my saliva off to 23 and me. The results...97.3% Ashkenazi Jew...99.7% European and .3% Eastern Asian & Native American. Not all that surprising except the .3%. The more important information came when she ran my results through an algorithm to see my genetic medical information. Yes we have a genetic component to our health but we have the ability to change. For example, my genetic type can not process bad high-fat foods. This can lead to high cholesterol and heart disease, both of which my mom suffered from. If I don't eat bad high-fat foods I can prevent this from happening to me. However good fats such as avocado and nuts are great for me to eat. This next thing completely blew my mind. When you have an autoimmune disease and a high inflammation level, the first thing doctors tell you to take is curcumin (tumeric). For some reason I never took it. I would stand in front of the tumeric supplements and powder every week at Whole Foods and think to myself how do I even use this? I couldn't figure it out so I never bought it. Maybe it was my intuition telling me to STAY AWAY. Why?? Because it is poison for someone with my genetic type. I could probably write an entire book on all of this information...so stay tuned. I guess I wonder why more doctors don't use this. It would make it so much easier to treat their patients. No guess work involved. As I have tried to be the healthiest version of myself, I have peeled back layer after layer to get to the root cause of my disease. I am on a mission and I will continue.

Everyones journey is unique

Why is my journey unique? Because it's mine. Everyone has their own unique personal journey. I wanted to put mine out there to help people. The most important lesson is… DO NOT become your illness. Just be you with a pesky illness. Whether you have an autoimmune disease, another chronic illness, are overweight or have suffered trauma and loss, I hope that you can relate.

Here is what I have learned. There is no one person that can put you on the path to a healthy lifestyle but you. I spent years going to doctors and hiring personal trainers, with no success. Why? I wanted them to just do it for me!! Well guess what? That doesn't work.

In April 2013, I went to see the Jillian Michaels' "Maximize Your Life Tour" at the Ferguson Center in Newport News, Virginia. She is inspiring, amazing and absolutely hysterical. She said one thing that was the game changer for me…"Find Your WHY!!" I looked at Chris and said to him "You and my kids are my WHY." They need a healthy version of me. They deserve a healthy version of me. Heck I deserve a healthy version of me. I needed to take control.

"The two most important days in your life are the day you are born and the day you find out WHY." Mark Twain

From that day in 2013 until now and forever, I will spend my time finding answers for me and anyone that needs my help. Our bodies give us subtle hints when things are off kilter. We must listen to them. We must take control to heal ourselves before our bodies get so frustrated that they give us a BIG sign.

I do still believe there is a place for traditional medicine, as long as we can get to the root cause, and combine it with alternative medicine. I always turn first to alternative. I start everyday with immune-supporting antioxidants, supplements and essential oils as well as organic or locally grown food and exercise.

A healthy journey is a lifestyle change and a mind shift. It doesn't take a rocket scientist to figure it out (although when I was in the WW meetings I thought it did). There is no before and after picture. Love the body you have every single day. It is the only one you get and it is beautiful. The beauty is that we all look different. The journey never ends. Mind shift...this journey is fun. Yummy food, fun exercise and feeling good. There is nothing better then waking up every morning feeling happy and healthy. For me this is an absolute blessing as I spent many years feeling the opposite.

I hope my story resonates with you. I am here for you. I am here to listen and support you. I am a holistic health coach, Young Living essential oil educator and real person who has struggled and still struggles. I hope to hear from each and every one of my readers.

I love you all and thank you for taking the time to read my story.

Stef
xoxo
email: stef@finallyfitforever.net
website: finallyfitforever.net

A week in the life of Stef

B efore I go into what I do every day, remember everyone is an individual. I just want to give you an idea of how I live my life everyday. You need to find out what works for you.

Every morning I start with an antioxidant drink, called Ningxia red and supplements, along with my essential oils. Oils to support my hormones, joy over my heart, highest potential on my solar plexus, stress away on the back of my neck, an oil to support my thyroid on my neck and various other oils. I always like to put positive thoughts and intentions into the universe and these oils help me do that. Breakfast is next. I eat oatmeal banana bread (recipe to follow) and a cup of coffee with lactose free cream. I love this bread and I can eat the same thing every day. I'm trying to branch out.

After my workout I eat the rest of my bread. Lunch is usually a salad with hardboiled egg, edamame and a salad or hummus and a kale salad, and always fruit. Mid-afternoon snack is a cacao quinoa energy bar or nuts. Dinner is always a salad and tons of vegetables, sometimes fish, sometimes a red lentil pattie. I love quinoa or red lentil pasta with veggies and tomato sauce. Evening snack is a must to keep me on track. I LOVE ice cream, so I have found two that I can eat, Arctic Zero and Wink. I do like a small piece of organic dark chocolate over 72% sometimes as well. This is just a small sample.

I love my workout regimen. Monday and Wednesday I drive the 35 minutes to Chesapeake to work out with Jared. He is forever changing my workouts. I can assure you when I leave and get in my car I have to sit and catch my breath for about ten minutes. Tuesday and Thursday I do an hour gentle yoga class. Friday, Saturday and Sunday, sometimes all three or just one or two, I go to the local recreation center for cardio workouts. I try to stretch every day-this is my weakness and I need to get more committed to it. I also love to ride my bike at the Oceanfront and walk my dogs. The more I move the better my joints feel. I believe in self-care. I get massages, facials and pedicures. They are therapeutic and necessary to feed my soul. The next stop on my personal journey is to meditate more. I am going to start with some guided meditation, as I diffuse my intention setting oils. If we don't take care of ourselves, no one else will.

"Nuturing yourself is not selfish - it's essential to your survival and your well-being." Renee Peterson Trudeau

Chris Freeman's special bread

18 ounce container of organic oats plus 1 cup
2 TBS cinnamon*
1 TBS baking powder
2 TBS stevia*
1/2 tsp salt

5 large or 6 small very ripe bananas
1 16oz container of organic egg whites
1 4oz container of organic plain greek yogurt
1 TBS vanilla

Preheat oven to 360 degrees. In a food processor or blender grind the oatmeal to a chunky flour texture, some of the oats will stay whole and this is fine. In a large bowl combine all dry ingredients and mix thoroughly. Combine all wet ingredients in blender and blend until bananas are smooth Combine all the ingredients and mix thoroughly. Spray 5 small loaf pans with organic coconut spray. Spread mixture evenly in the loaf pans. Bake for 34 minutes at 360 degrees on convection bake.

*increase or decrease cinnamon and stevia to your preference